Better Bass With..

Rockschool

Welcome to Bass Grade 3	2
Bass Guitar Tablature Explained	3

Pieces:

Manic	4
Ruff Daddy	6
Yoakam's Hokum	8
Grade 3 In The U.K.	10
Xaminer Blues II	12
BC/DC	14
Technical Exercises	16
Sight Reading	18
Improvisation & Interpretation	18
Ear Tests	19
General Musicianship Questions	20
The Guru's Guide	21

A *Rockschool* Publication
Broomfield House, Broomfield Road, Richmond, Surrey TW9 3HS

Welcome To *Bass* Grade 3

Welcome to the Rockschool *Bass* Grade 3 pack. The book and CD contain everything needed to play bass in this grade. In the book you will find the exam scores in both standard notation and TAB. The CD has full stereo mixes of each tune, backing tracks to play along with for practice and tuning notes. Handy tips on playing the pieces and the marking schemes can be found in the Guru's Guide on page 21. If you have any queries about this or any other Rockschool exam, please call us on **020 8332 6303** or email us at office@rockschool.co.uk or visit our website http://www.rockschool.co.uk. Good luck!

Player Zone Techniques in Grade 2 and Grade 3

The eight Rockschool grades are divided into four Zones. *Bass* Grade 3, along with Grade 2, is part of the *Player Zone*. This Zone is for those of you who are building on key skills to express your musical personality across a range of styles.

Grade 2: in this grade you are beginning to acquire a range of physical and expressive techniques, including palm damping and the use of double stops on adjacent strings, simple legato and staccato, slides, vibrato, hammer ons and pull offs. It is in this grade that you will be able to begin work on developing your stylistic appreciation

Grade 3: this grade continues the foundation work laid in the previous grade. As a player you will be encountering syncopated eighth and 16th notes, slides, bends and vibrato. You will also be starting to develop a sense of volume contrasts (dynamics) in your playing. The pieces of music now cover 2 pages and you will be encountering faster speeds than in previous grades.

Player Zone Bass Exams

There are **three** types of exam that can be taken using this pack: Grade Exam, Performance Certificate and Band Exam.

- **Bass Grade 3 Exam: this is for players who want to develop performance and technical skills**

Players wishing to enter for a *Bass* Grade 3 exam need to prepare **three** pieces, of which **one** may be a free choice piece chosen from outside the printed repertoire. In addition, you must prepare the technical exercises in this book, undertake either a sight reading test or an improvisation & interpretation test, take an ear test and answer general musicianship questions. Samples of these are printed in the book.

- ***Player Zone* Performance Certificate in Bass: this is for players who want to focus on performing in a range of styles**

To enter for your *Player Zone* Performance Certificate you play pieces only. You can choose any **five** of the six tunes printed in this book, or you can bring in up to **two** free choice pieces as long as they meet the standards set out in the Guru's Guide below.

- ***Player Zone* Band Exam in Bass, Guitar and Drums: this is for players who want to play as a band**

The *Player Zone* Band Exam is for all of you who are in a group, and features guitar, bass and drums. You play together in the exam, using the parts printed in the Guitar, Bass and Drum books. Like the *Player Zone* Performance Certificate, you play **five** of the six printed pieces, or you can include up to **two** free choice pieces as long as they meet the standards set out in the Guru's Guide below. If you take this exam you will be marked as a unit with each player expected to contribute equally to the overall performance of each piece played.

Bass Guitar Tablature Explained
Bass Guitar music in this book is notated in both standard notation and tablature

THE MUSICAL STAVE shows pitches and rhythms and is divided by lines into bars. Pitches are named after the first seven letters of the alphabet.

TABLATURE graphically represents the bass guitar fingerboard. Each horizontal line represents a string, and each number represents a fret.

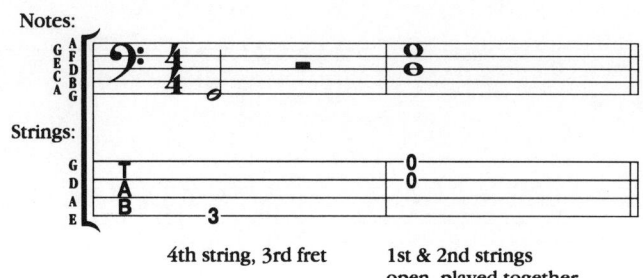

4th string, 3rd fret   1st & 2nd strings open, played together

Definitions For Special Bass Guitar Notation

HAMMER ON: Pick the lower note, then sound the higher note by fretting it without picking.

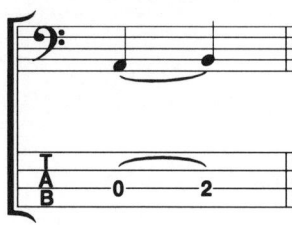

PULL OFF: Pick the higher note then sound the lower note by lifting the finger without picking.

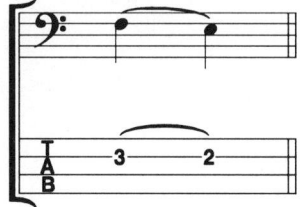

SLIDE: Pick the first note, then slide to the next with the same finger.

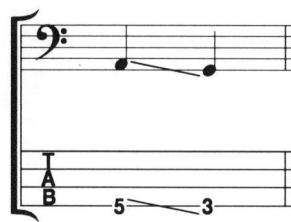

GLISSANDO: Pick the note and slide along the string in the direction indicated.

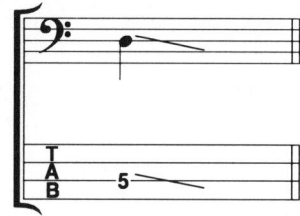

THUMB SLAP: Strike the indicated note with the thumb, in a percussive manner.

PULL: 'Pop' the note by quickly pulling the string upward (usually with the index finger) and releasing it.

DEAD (GHOST) NOTES: Pick the string while the note is muted with the fretting hand.

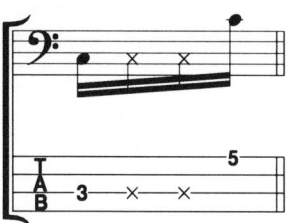

NATURAL HARMONICS: Lightly touch the string above the indicated fret then pick to sound a harmonic.

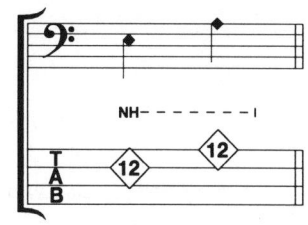

- (accent) • Accentuate note (play it louder).
- (accent) • Accentuate note with great intensity. 
- (staccato) • Shorten time value of note. 
- ■ • Downstroke
- V • Upstroke

D.%. al Coda

D.C. al Fine

tacet

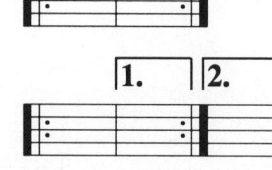

- Go back to the sign (%), then play until the bar marked *To Coda* ⊕ then skip to the section marked ⊕ *Coda*.
- Go back to the beginning of the song and play until the bar marked *Fine* (end).
- Instrument is silent (drops out).
- Repeat bars between signs.
- When a repeated section has different endings, play the first ending only the first time and the second ending only the second time.

Manic

Simon Eyre

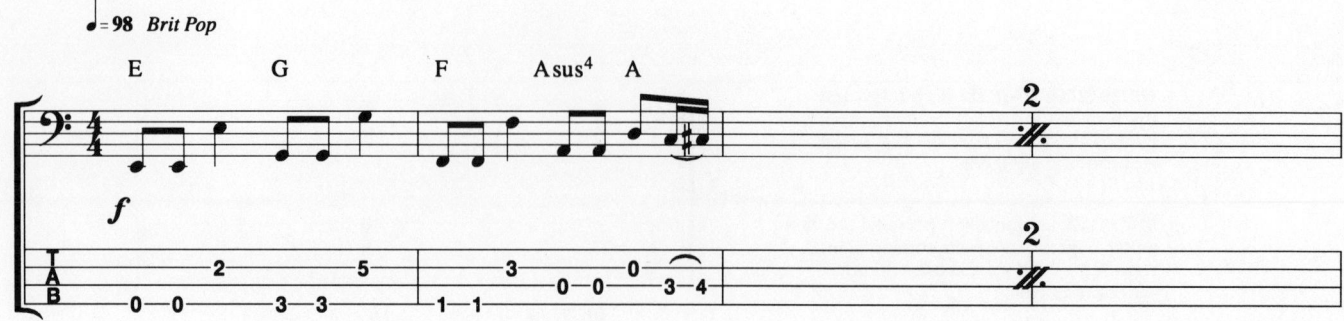
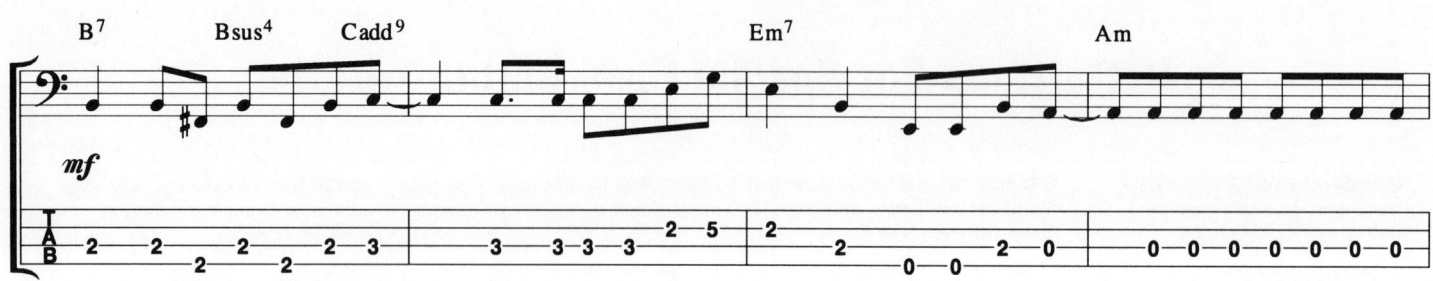
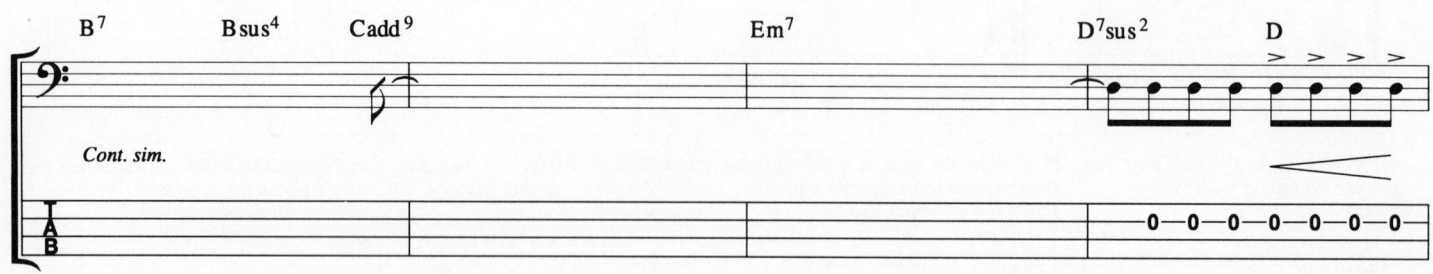
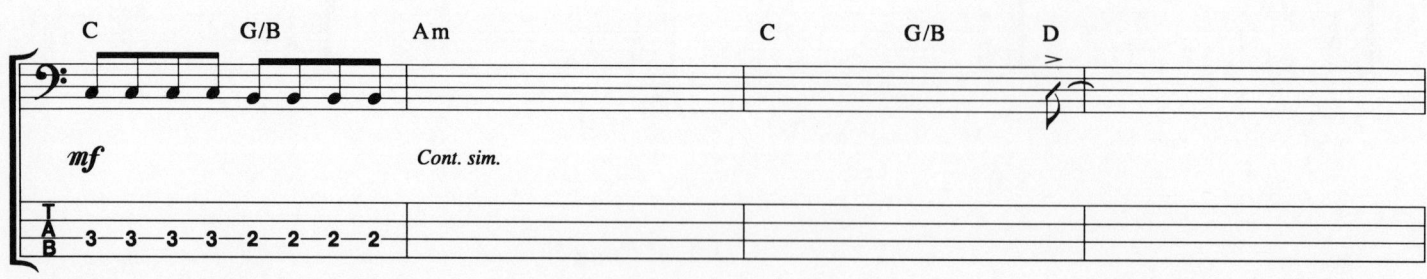
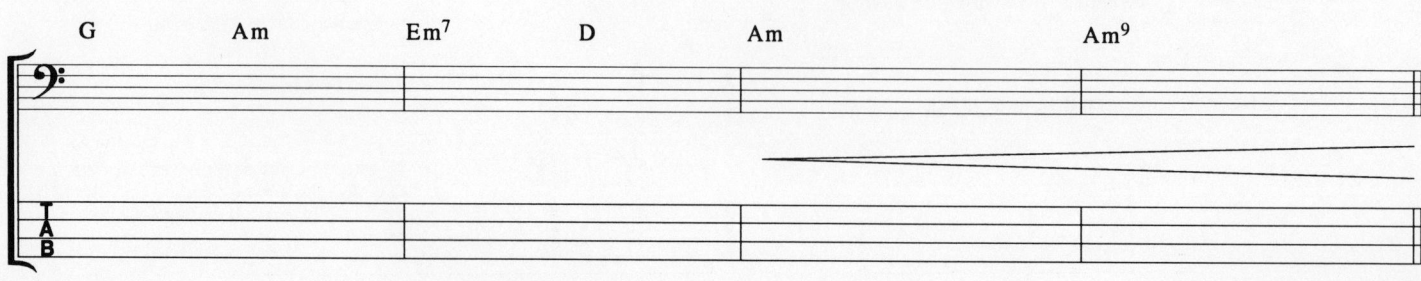

© 1998 by Rock School Ltd.

This music is copyright. Photocopying is illegal

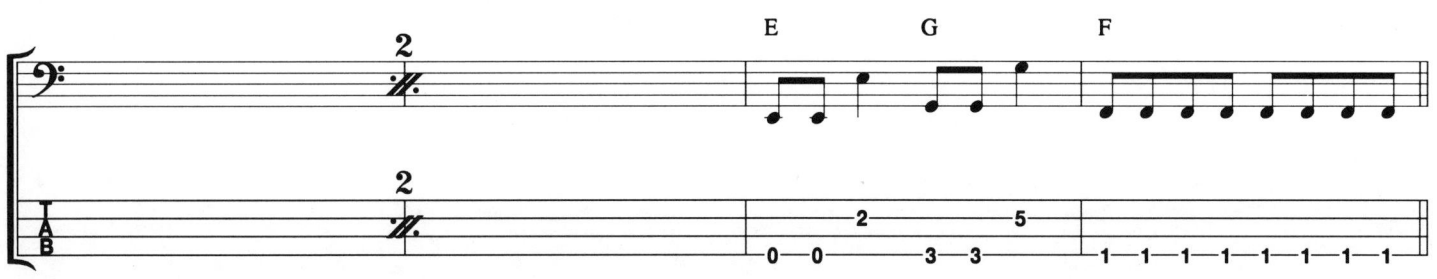
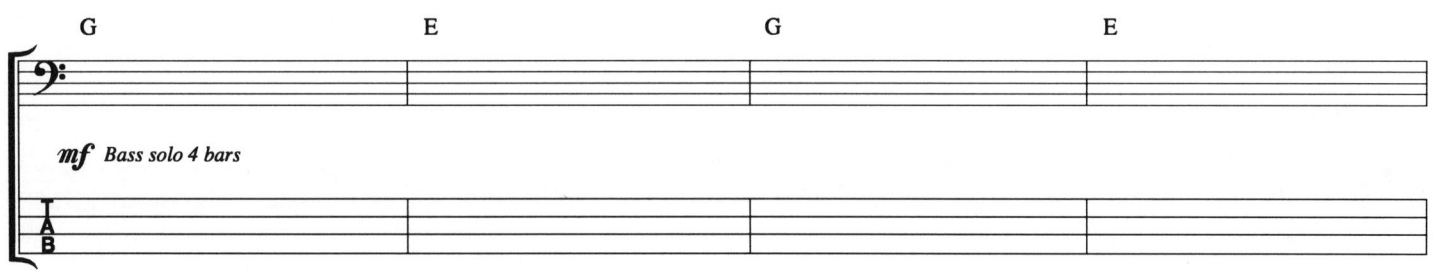
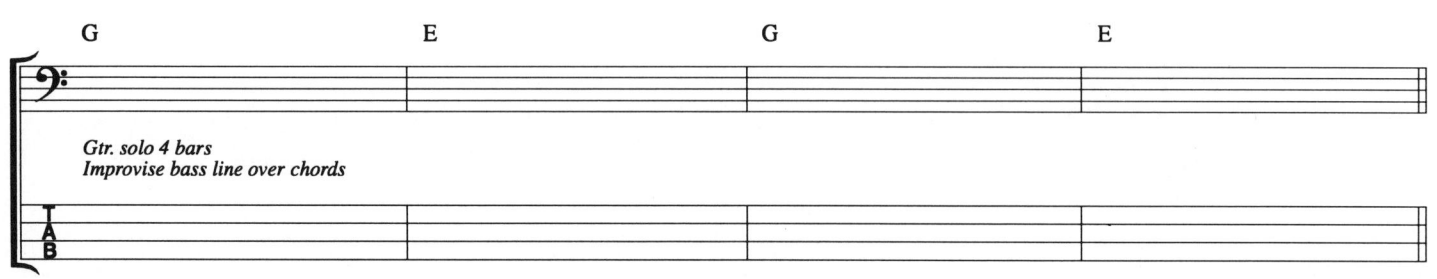

Ruff Daddy

Adrian York

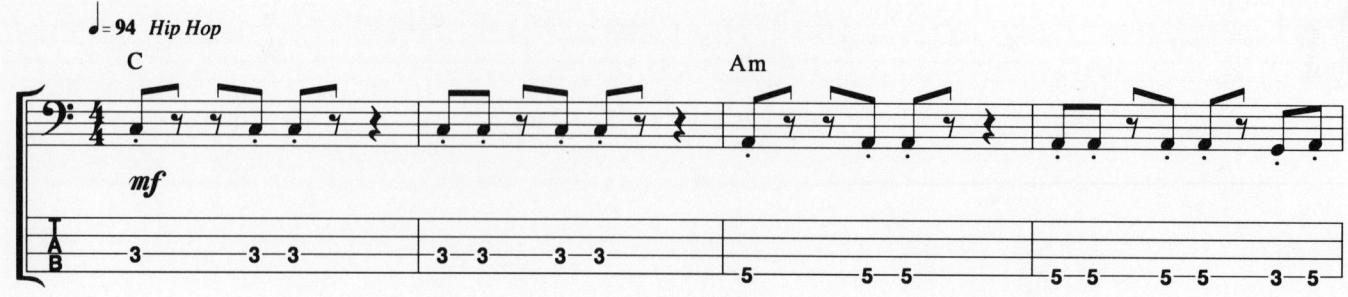
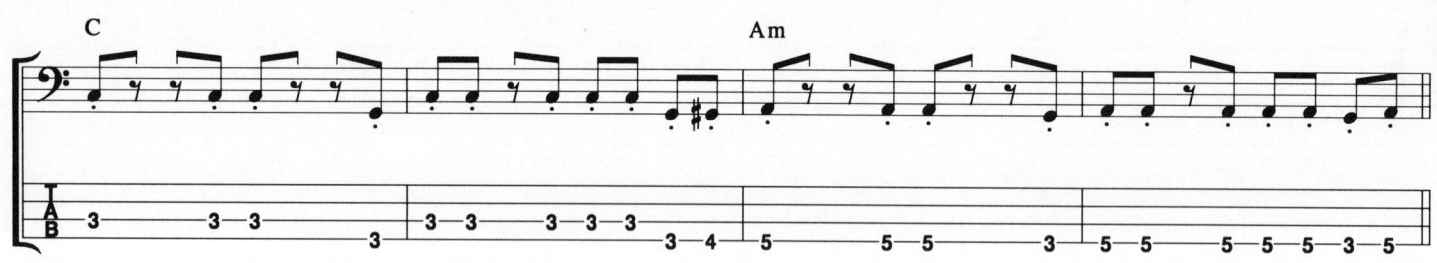
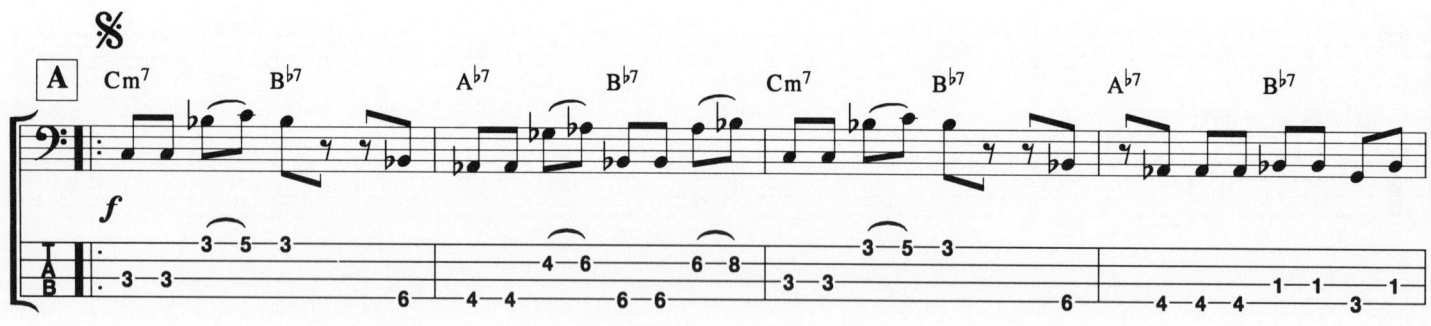
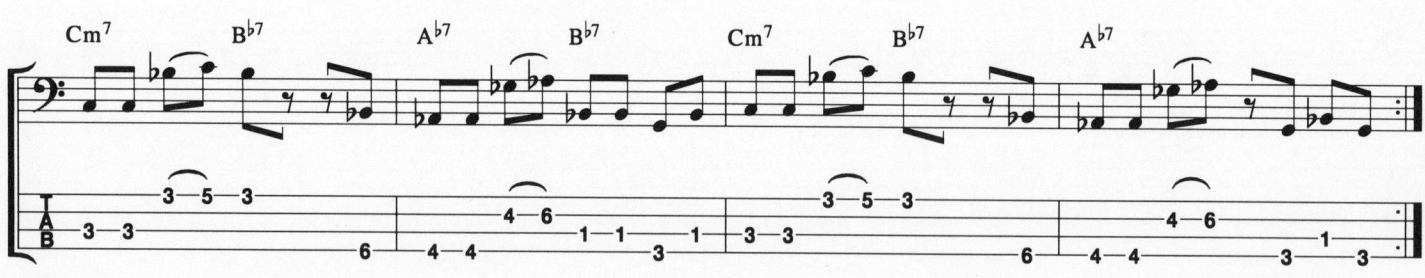
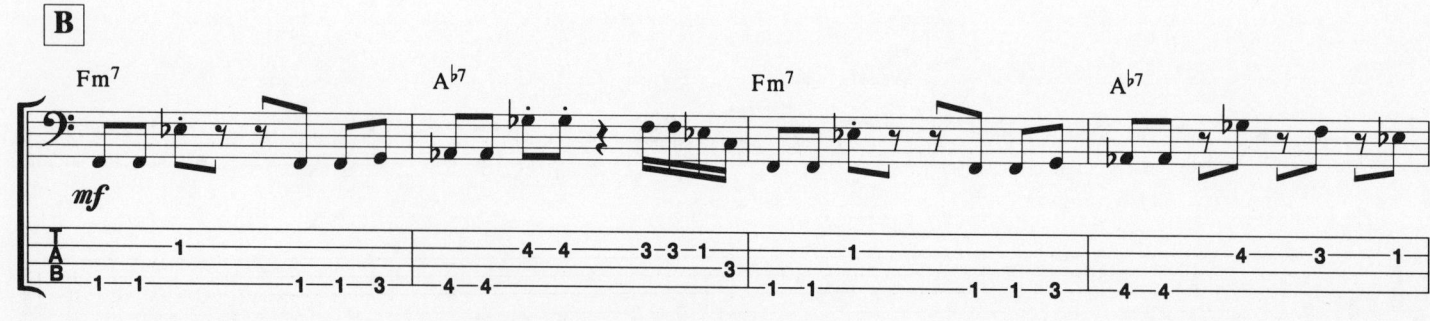

© 1998 by Rock School Ltd.

This music is copyright. Photocopying is illegal

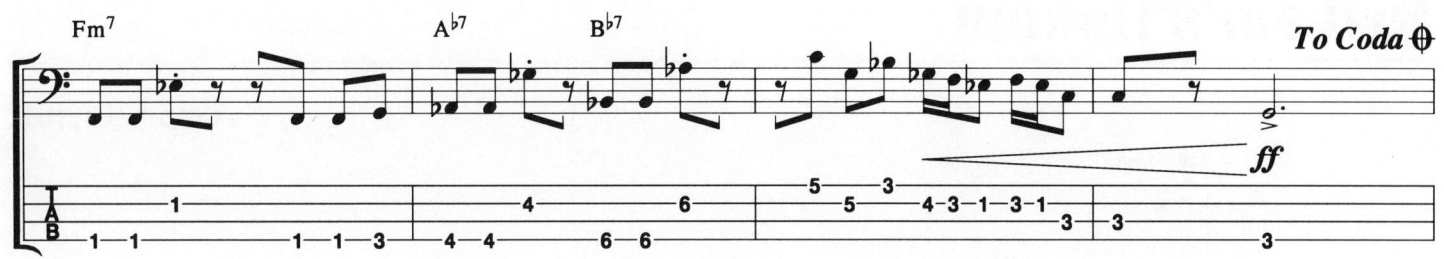

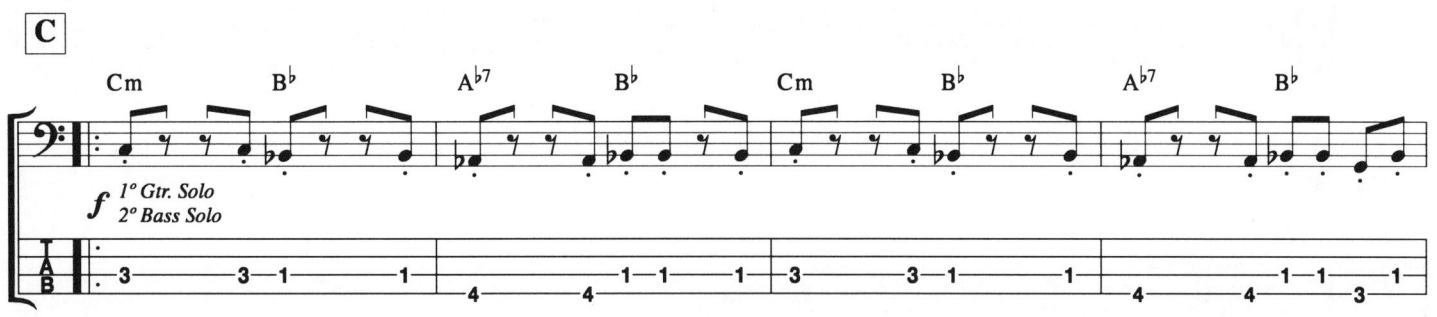

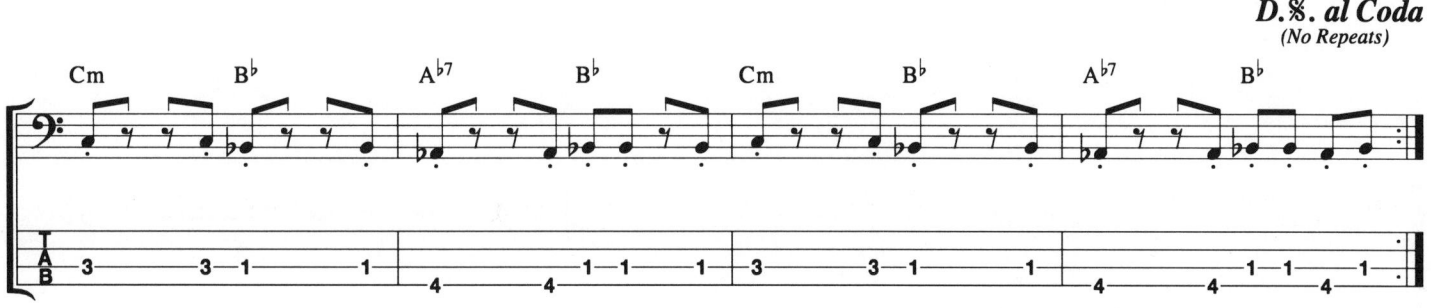

Yoakam's Hokum

Alison Rayner

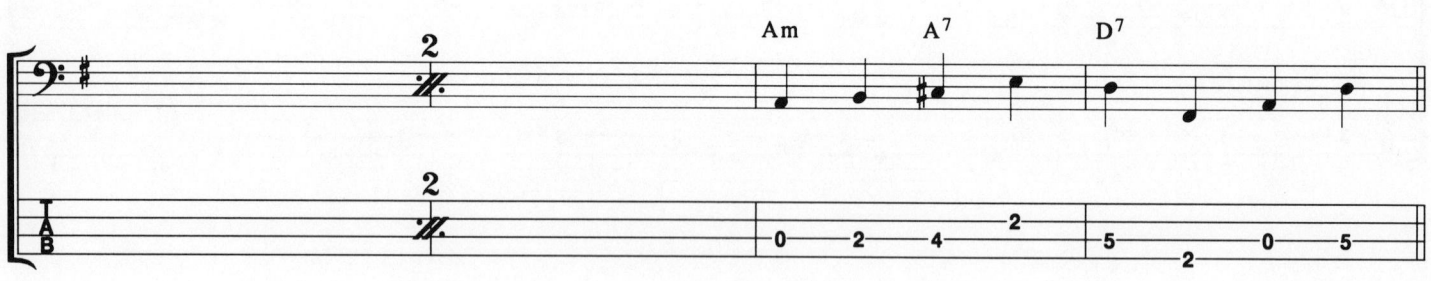

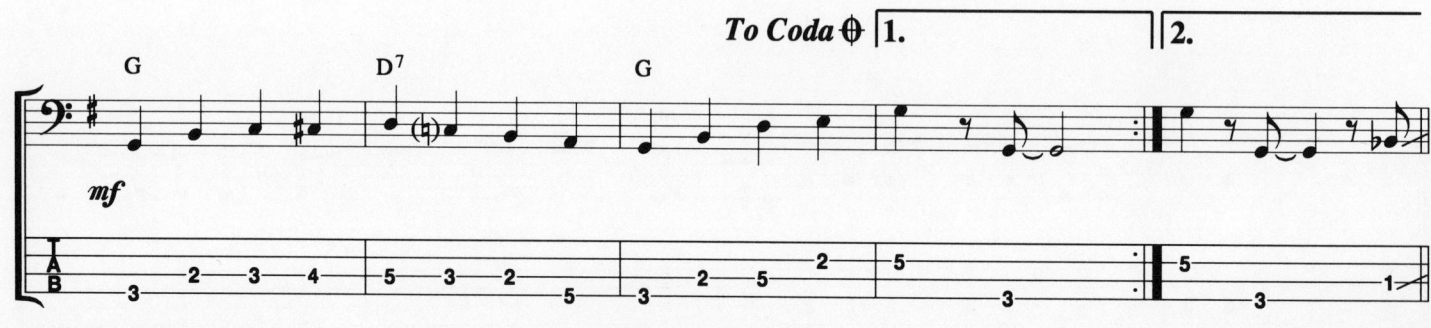

© 1998 by Rock School Ltd.

This music is copyright. Photocopying is illegal

B
G6
A7
D7
C7
A
D
G
D.𝄋. al Coda
Coda
G
A
D
p
mp
G
F♯ G
mf
f

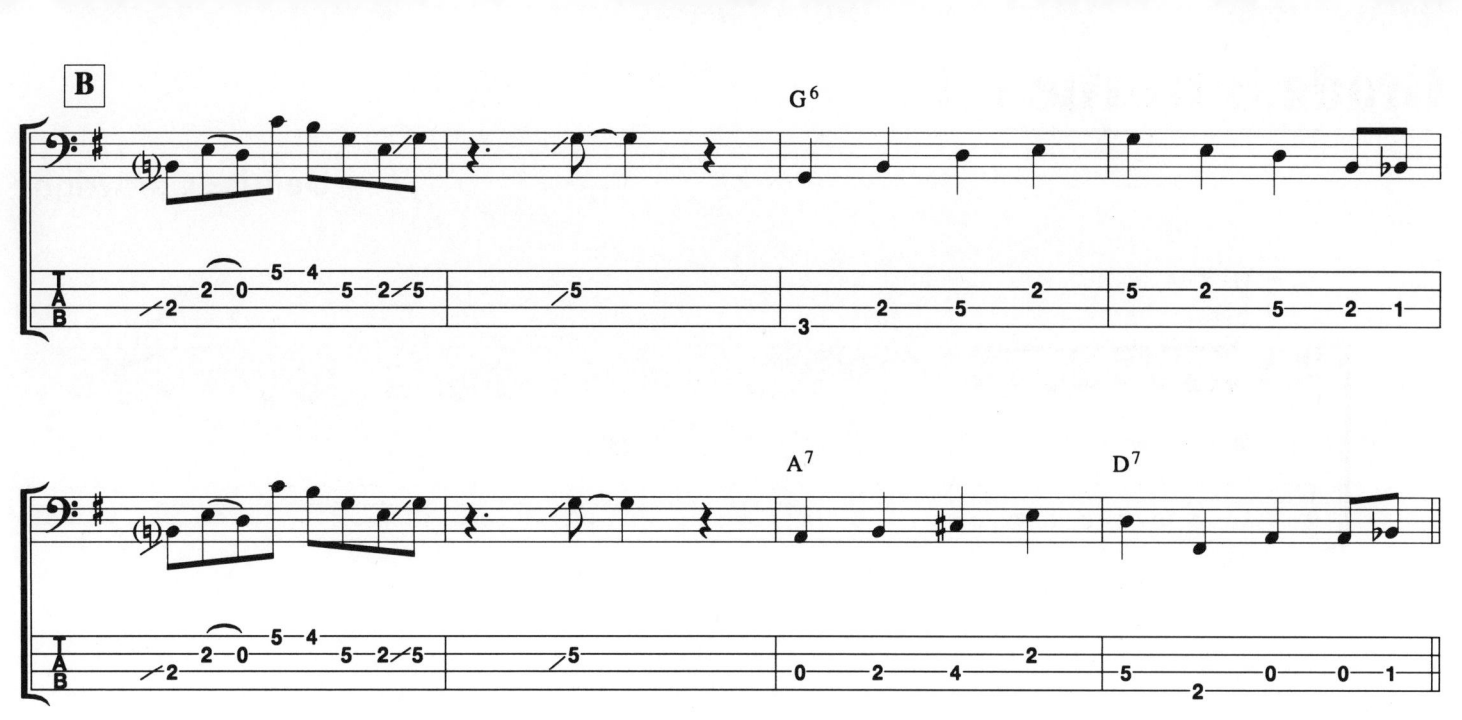

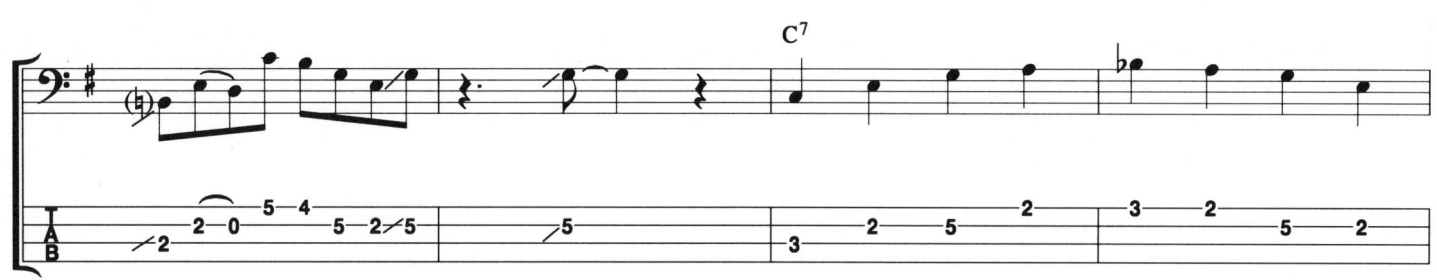

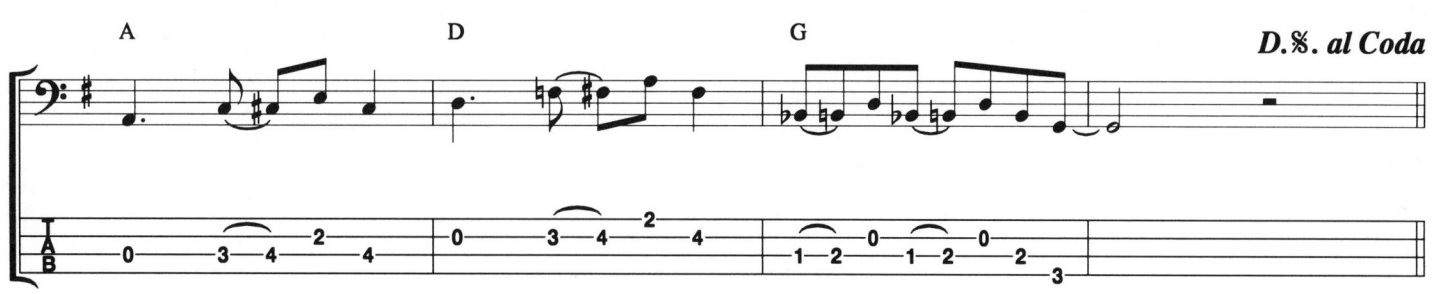

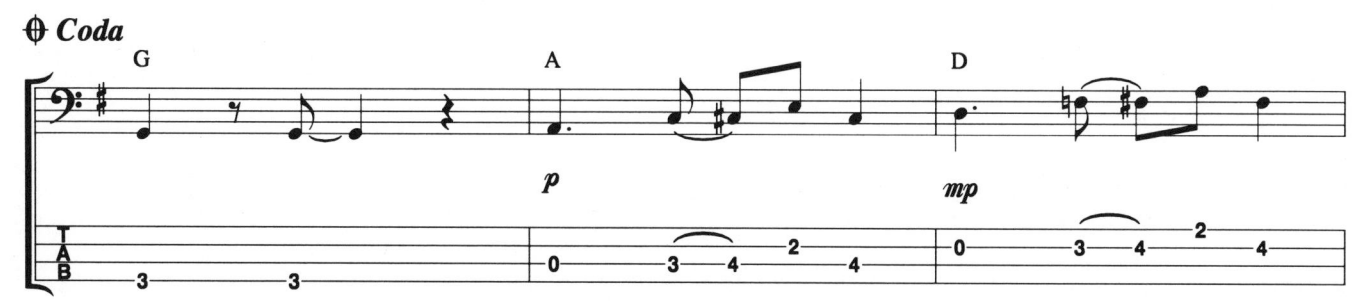

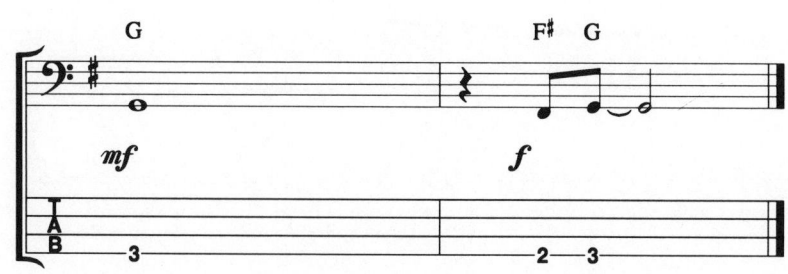

Grade 3 In The U.K.

Deirdre Cartwright

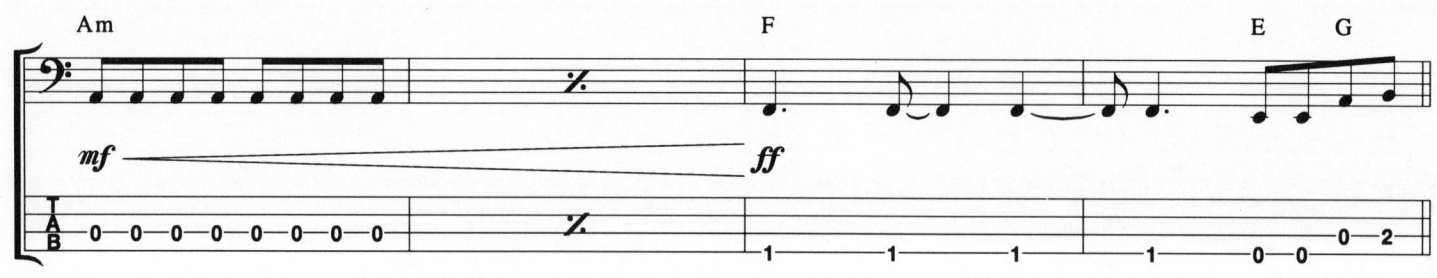

© 1998 by Rock School Ltd.   This music is copyright. Photocopying is illegal

Xaminer Blues II

Deirdre Cartwright

BC/DC

Deirdre & Bernice Cartwright

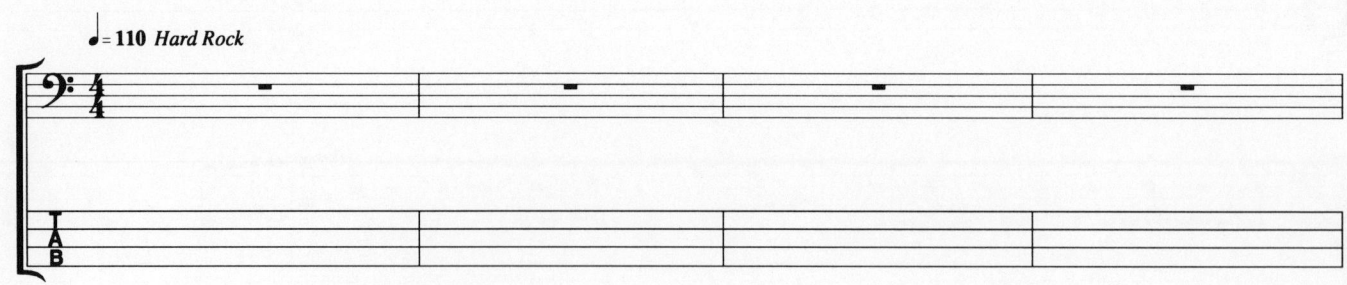
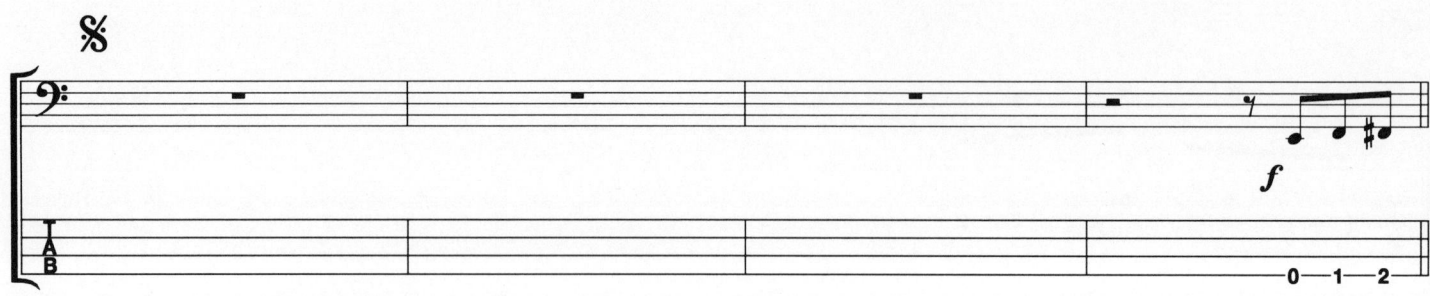
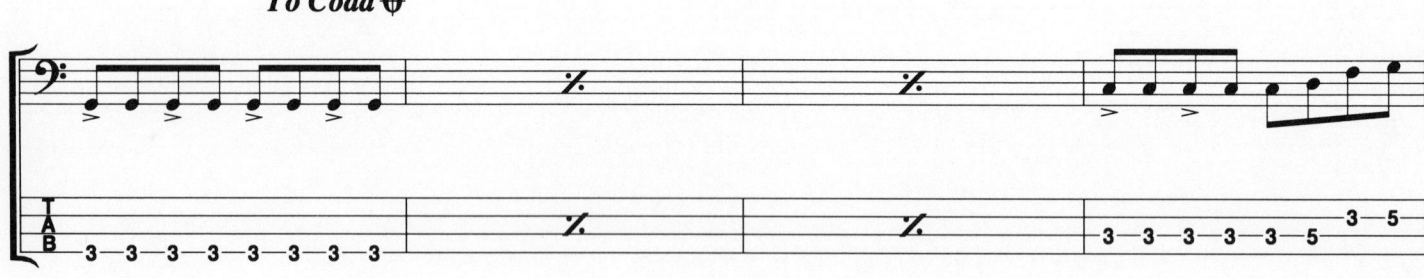
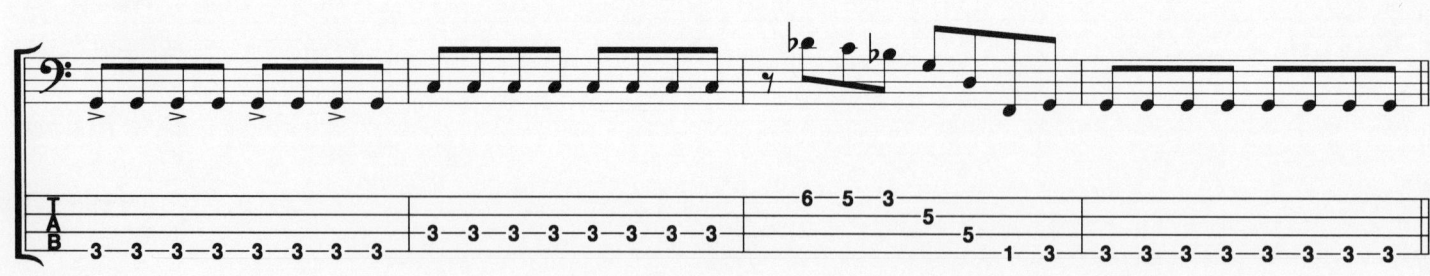

© 1998 by Rock School Ltd.

This music is copyright. Photocopying is illegal

Technical Exercises

In this section, the examiner will ask you to play a selection of exercises drawn from each of the three groups shown below. These exercises contain examples of the kinds of scales and arpeggios you can use when playing the pieces. You do not need to memorise the exercises (and can use the book in the exam) but the examiner will be looking for the speed of your response. The examiner will also give credit for the level of your musicality.

The exercises should be prepared in all of the following keys: C, F, G, B♭, D, D♭ and A.
The exercises should be played at ♩ = 90. The examiner will give you this tempo in the exam.

Group A: Arpeggios

1. Major 7th arpeggios. B♭ major 7th example shown.

2. Dominant 7th arpeggios. B♭ dominant 7th example shown.

3. Minor 7th arpeggios. B♭ minor 7th example shown.

4. Minor 7th ♭5 arpeggios. B♭ minor 7th ♭5 example shown.

Group B: Scales

1. Major scales. B♭ major example shown.

Group C: Intervals

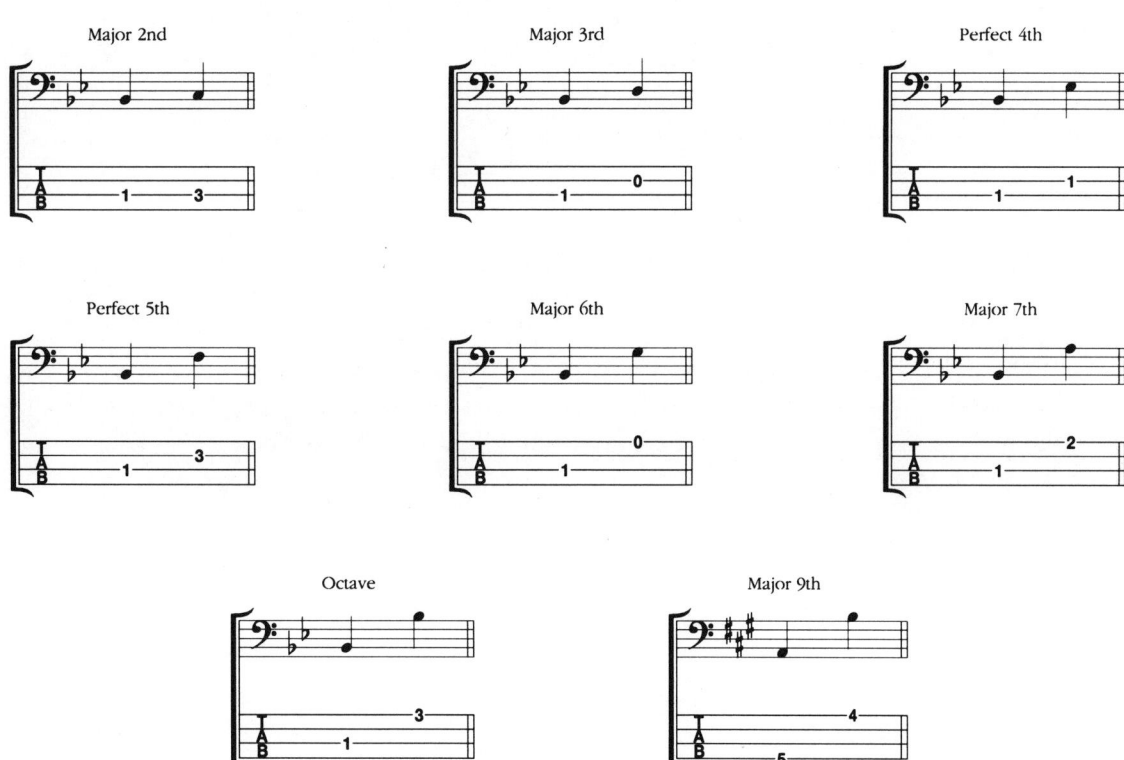

Sight Reading *or* Improvisation & Interpretation

In this section you have a choice between either a sight reading test or an improvisation & interpretation test. Printed below is an example of the type of **sight reading** test you are likely to encounter in the exam. This will be in one of the following styles: blues, rock, funk or jazz. The examiner will allow you 90 seconds to prepare it and will set the tempo for you on a metronome.

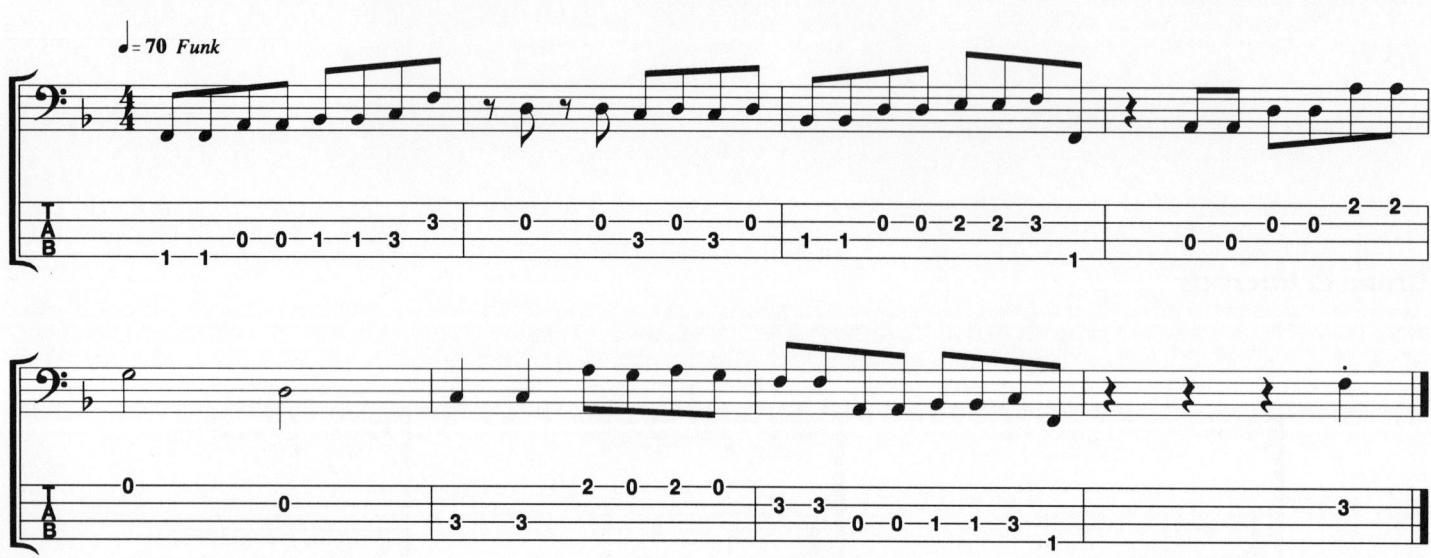

Printed below is an example of the type of **improvisation & interpretation** test you are likely to encounter in an exam. You will be asked to play an improvised line over a set of chord changes lasting 8 bars in one of the following styles: blues, rock, funk or jazz. The examiner will allow you 90 seconds to prepare it and will set the tempo for you on a metronome.

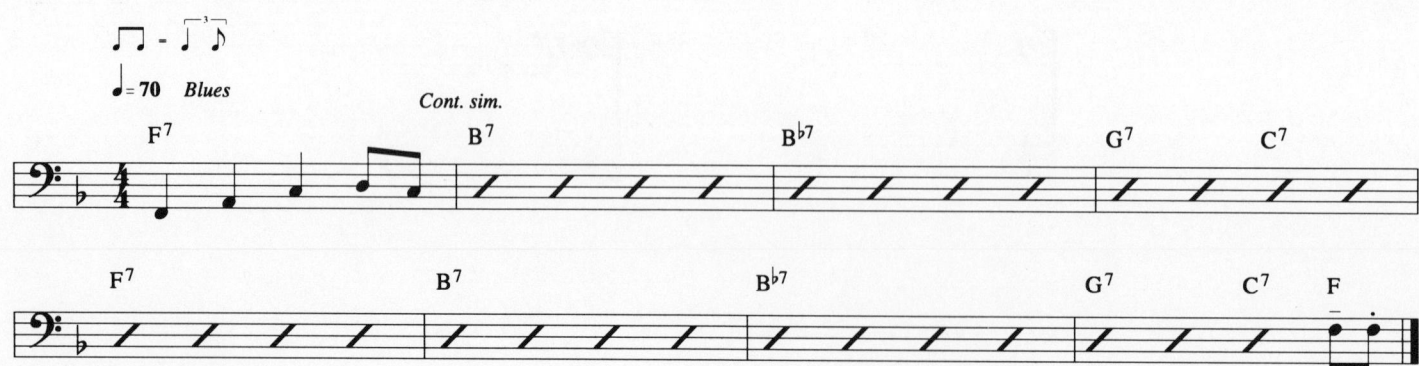

Ear Tests

You will find two ear tests in this grade. The examiner will play each test to you twice on CD. You will find two examples of the type of test you will get in the exam printed below.

Test 1

You will be asked to play back on your bass a simple melody of not more than four bars composed from the notes E, G, A, B and D (Quarter and Eighth notes only). Players will be given the tonic note and will hear the sequence twice.

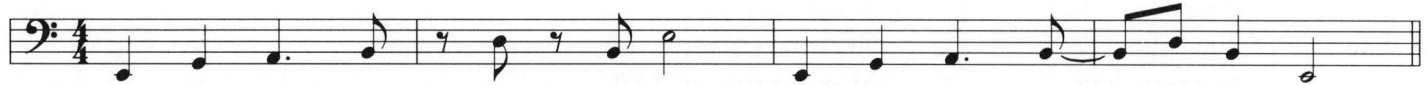

Test 2

You will also be asked to recognise a four chord sequence using chords from the following: I, IV and V in the keys of either E major, A major, C major or F major. You will hear the sequence twice and you may use your bass as a guide while the sequence is playing. An example in C major is shown below.

General Musicianship Questions

You will be asked five General Musicianship Questions at the end of the exam.

Topics:

i) Music theory
ii) Knowledge of the candidate's instrument

The music theory questions will cover the following topics at this grade:

> Recognition of pitches   Dynamic markings (p, mp, mf and f)
> Note values   Repeat markings
> Rests   Cresc. and dim.
> Time signatures   Accents, staccato, vibrato
> Key signatures   Hammer ons, pull offs
> D.S. and D.C. al coda

Knowledge of the construction of the following chord types:

> Major   Major 7th   Dominant 7th
> Minor   Minor 7th   Minor 7th♭5

Questions on these topics will be drawn from one of the pieces played you have played in the exam.

The instrument knowledge questions will cover the following topics at this grade:

> Plugging into the amplifier and the bass
> Volume and tone adjustments on the bass
> Volume and tone adjustments on the amplifier

Knowledge of parts of the bass guitar:

> Fretboard, neck, body, tuning pegs, nut, pickups,
> bridge, pickup selectors, scratchplate, and jack socket

Knowledge of main bass makes

The Guru's Guide To *Bass* Grade 3

This section contains some handy hints compiled by Rockschool's Bass Guru to help you get the most out of the performance pieces. Do feel free to adapt the tunes to suit your playing style. Remember, these tunes are your chance to show your musical imagination and personality.

The TAB fingerings are suggestions only. Feel free to use different neck positions as they suit you. Please also note the solos featured in the full mixes are not meant to be indicative of the standard required for the grade.

Bass Grade 3 Tunes

Rockschool tunes help you play the hit tunes you enjoy. The pieces have been written by top pop and rock composers and players according to style specifications drawn up by Rockschool.

The tunes printed here are divided into two groups of three pieces. The first group of pieces belongs to the *contemporary mainstream* and features current styles in today's charts. The second group of pieces consists of *roots styles*, those classic grooves and genres which influence every generation of performers.

CD full mix track 1, backing track 8: *Manic*

A strong piece written in the style of the early Manic Street Preachers. This piece requires accurate picking hand technique to cover the accented pedal tones of the opening four bars. Otherwise the part is quite straightforward and uses mainly open positions. There is a bass solo marked from bars 29-36.

Composer: Simon Eyre. Simon has played for a number of top names including the Lighthouse Family, Paul Weller, Chaka Khan and Jim Diamond.

CD full mix track 2, backing track 9: *Ruff Daddy*

This uses a pared down riff and hip hop groove similar in style to Puff Daddy's *I'll be Missing You*. This part starts with stabbed notes which accent the guitar riff, and continues throughout, so watch out for the rests. A bass solo is marked at [C].

Composer: Adrian York. Adrian has played with many famous artists such as Sandie Shaw, Jimmy Ruffin, Paul Young and Lily Savage, and is the author of the *Style File* series.

CD full mix track 3, backing tack 10: *Yoakam's Hokum*

This piece took its inspiration (and its title) from modern country players such as Dwight Yoakam. This part is quite straightforward and uses mainly quarter and eighth notes. There is no solo marked but the repeats should be ad libbed as required.

Composer: Alison Rayner. Alison is equally at home with either electric or upright bass and has backed such luminaries as the late Tal Farlow and U.K. jazz guitar virtuoso John Etheridge.

CD full mix track 4, backing track 11: *Grade 3 in the U.K.*

This track bears a strong resemblance to The Jam in their prime. At 144 bpm, this is the quickest piece in the grade and features mainly pedal eighth notes with some octave jumps. This will sound great played with a pick.

Composer: Deirdre Cartwright. Deirdre fronted the TV *Rockschool* series in the 1980's and now plays and teachers extensively throughout Europe.

CD full mix track 5, backing track 12: *Xaminer Blues II*

A blues song in the style of John Mayall or early Fleetwood Mac. This is another piece to feature pedal bass passages, with a few eighth note triplets played in unison with the guitar part. Some ad libbing is required at [C].

Composer: Deirdre Cartwright:

CD full mix track 6, backing track 13: *BC/DC*

Hard rock in the style of Deep Purple (check out their (in)famous *Smoke on the Water*). The lines are mainly straightforward, combining pedal eighth notes and unison passages. This is another song in which the bass needs to be both bold and driving.

Composers: Bernice and Deirdre Cartwright.

CD Musicians:
   Guitars: Deirdre Cartwright **Bass:** Geoff Gascoyne **Drums:** Steve Creese
   Keyboards and programming: Adrian York

Grade Exam Marking Scheme

The table below shows the marking scheme for the *Bass* Grade 3 exam.

ELEMENT	PASS	MERIT	DISTINCTION
Piece 1 Piece 2 Piece 3	13 out of 20 13 out of 20 13 out of 20	15 out of 20 15 out of 20 15 out of 20	17+ out of 20 17+ out of 20 17+ out of 20
Technical Exercises	11 out of 15	12 out of 15	13+ out of 15
Either: Sight Reading *Or:* Improvisation & Interpretation	6 out of 10	7 out of 10	8+ out of 10
Ear Tests	6 out of 10	7 out of 10	8+ out of 10
General Musicianship Questions	3 out of 5	4 out of 5	5 out of 5
Total Marks	**Pass: 65% +**	**Pass: 75% +**	**Pass: 85% +**

Player Zone Performance Certificate/Band Exam Marking Scheme

The table below shows the marking scheme for both the *Player Zone* Performance Certificate and the *Player Zone* Band Exam. You will see that the Pass mark for both is now **70%**. The Merit mark is **80%** and the mark for a Distinction performance is **90%**.

ELEMENT	PASS	MERIT	DISTINCTION
Piece 1	14 out of 20	16 out of 20	18+ out of 20
Piece 2	14 out of 20	16 out of 20	18+ out of 20
Piece 3	14 out of 20	16 out of 20	18+ out of 20
Piece 4	14 out of 20	16 out of 20	18+ out of 20
Piece 5	14 out of 20	16 out of 20	18+ out of 20
Total Marks	**Pass: 70% +**	**Merit: 80% +**	**Distinction: 90% +**

Free Choice Song Criteria

You can bring in your own performance pieces to play in any of the exams featured. In the Grade Exams you can bring in **one** piece.

In either the *Player Zone* Performance Certificate or the *Player Zone* First Band Exam you may bring in up to **two** pieces. You should read the following criteria carefully.

- Players may bring in either their own compositions or songs already in the public domain, including hits from the charts.
- Songs may be performed either solo or to a CD or tape backing track.
- Players should bring in two copies of the piece to be performed, notated either in standard notation, chord charts or TAB. Players must use an original copy of the tune to be performed, and must provide a second copy for the examiner, which may be a photocopy. For copyright reasons, photocopies handed to the examiner will be retained and destroyed by Rock School in due course.
- Players may perform either complete songs or extracts: such as a solo part.
- Players should aim to keep their free choice songs below 2 minutes in length.
- *Player Zone* Band Exam parts should feature independent lines for all instruments.
- Players should aim to make each free choice song of a technical standard similar to those published in the Rockschool *Bass* Grade 3 book. However, examiners will be awarding credit for how well you perform the song. In general players should aim to play songs that mix the following physical and expressive techniques and rhythm skills:

Physical Techniques: accurate left and right hand co-ordination; picking hand damping; alternate picking, use of double stops on adjacent strings, damping for percussive sounds, use of syncopated eighth and 16th note feels.

Expressive Techniques: legato and staccato, dynamics (soft to loud), slides, fretting hand legato, hammer-ons and pull-offs, accented notes, controlled bends, use of blues and pentatonic scales in solos.

Rhythm Skills: songs should contain a mixture of whole, half, quarter, eighth and 16th notes, dotted quarter notes and their associated rests. Songs should contain simple uses of syncopation and be in 4/4 time signatures.

You, or your teacher, may wish to adapt an existing piece of music to suit the criteria above. You should ensure that any changes to the music are clearly marked on the sheet submitted to the examiner.

Entering Rockschool Exams

Entering a Rockschool exam is easy, whether for the Grade, the *Player Zone* Performance certificate or the *Player Zone* Band Exam. Please read through these instructions carefully before filling in the exam entry form. Information on current exam fees can be obtained from Rock School by ringing **020 8332 6303**

- You should enter for the exam of your choice when you feel ready.

- You can enter for any one of three examination periods. These are shown below with their closing dates.

PERIOD	DURATION	CLOSING DATE
Period A	1st February to 15th March	1st December
Period B	15th May to 31st July	1st April
Period C	1st November to 15th December	1st October

These dates will apply from 1st January 1999 until further notice

- Please fill in the form giving your name, address and phone number. Please tick the type and level of exam, along with the period and year. Finally, fill in the fee box with the appropriate amount. You should send this form with a cheque or postal order to: **Rockschool, Broomfield House, 10 Broomfield Road, Richmond, Surrey TW9 3HS.**

- When you enter an exam you will receive from Rockschool an acknowledgement letter containing your exam entry number along with a copy of our exam regulations.

- Rockschool will allocate your entry to a centre and you will receive notification of the exam, showing a date, location and time as well as advice of what to bring to the centre.

- You should inform Rockschool of any cancellations or alterations to the schedule as soon as you can as it is usually not possible to transfer entries from one centre, or one period, to another without the payment of an additional fee.

- Please bring your music book and CD to the exam. You may not use photocopied music, nor the music used by someone else in another exam. The examiner will stamp each book after each session. You may be barred from taking an exam if you use someone else's music.

- You should aim to arrive for your *Bass* Grade 3 exam fifteen minutes before the time stated on the schedule.

- The exam centre will have a waiting area and warm-up facilities which you may use prior to being called into the main exam room.

- Each Rockschool Grade exam and *Player Zone* Performance Certificate is scheduled to last for 20 minutes. The *Player Zone* Band Exam will last 30 minutes. You can use a small proportion of this time to tune up and get ready.

- About 2 to 3 weeks after the exam you will receive a typed copy of the examiner's mark sheet. Every successful player will receive a Rockschool certificate of achievement.